SURVEY ANALYSIS OF MALE AND FEMALE INTIMATE RELATIONSHIPS: Its impact on university outcomes

I0409251

Peter Okoro Nwankwo, LL.M.; Ph. D

Albany State University

ISBN-13:978-1500148201

ISBN-10:1500148202

Create Space Publishers

TABLE OF CONTENTS   *Page iii*

ABSTRACT:

Friendship is a mutual affection among two or more people. Different cultures categorize friendships differently, and have different rules for how to fill those categories. In the present investigation, I analyze 371 questionnaires given to students in Nigeria. Unlike in the United States, in Nigeria the behavior of young adults is still monitored by parents. Thus, the results of this friendship survey are expected to be significantly different than a similar survey within the United States.

Results are summarized as follows.

Demographics and survey questions:

GPA by age

[18,25] year old students did better than average. Significance number was 0.089.

[26,35] year old students did worse than average. Significance number was 0.002.

[36,45] year old students did about average. Significance number was 0.257.

Adult child of an alcoholic?

On the average, children of alcoholics make lower grades than do others. Significance = 0.02. However, there are many children of alcoholics who do make average or better grades.

GPA by Religious practice pray

Those who make prayer their religious practice tend to make better grades than those who do not practice prayer.

Importance of religion in my life

Having religion be extremely important appears to be correlated with having average or near average grades. Significance = 0.05.

Having religion be only somewhat important or not at all important appears to be correlated with poor grades. Significance = 0.00.

However, many students still make average or better grades in spite of not considering religion to be important.

Childhood neighborhood

The Inner city child neighborhood can affect grade point average for students who otherwise would make average grade point average.

Have you ever sold drugs?

Having sold drugs is correlated with making poor grades.

However, not having sold drugs is not correlated with making good grades.

Have you ever belonged to a gang?

There is an association between having belonging to a gang and having poor grades.

However, not belonging to a gang is no assurance that you will make good grades.

How many of your current college close friends regularly smoke cigarettes?

Having all or most close friends smoke cigarettes is associated with making bad grades.

How do you think these friends would feel about you smoking cigarettes regularly?

Students who expect their close friends to approve of one self-smoking cigarettes are likely to make a low grade point average.

If you and your boy or girlfriend attend the same college or university, do you live or share an apartment or room together?

Living with your boy or girl friend appears to be significantly correlated with having an extremely low GPA.

Not living with your boy or girlfriend was not significantly correlated with any particular GPA.

Do you and your boyfriend have a baby together?

Having a baby together appears to be a handicap to making good grades.

However, not having a baby together is not assurance of making good grades.

Do you or your girlfriend have a baby together?

Having a baby together is significantly correlated with low grade point average.

Do you feel that you love your girlfriend vis vis as she you?

Those students who feel that love is mutual are more likely to make a grade point average in the average range, [3.5, 4.49].

What was your basis for choosing him/her for this intimate friendship?

Those student who said they chose beauty as a basis for intimate friendship are much more likely to have made a GPA in the range [1.6,2.4].

Have you ever been involved in a serious fight in which the police were called?

Those students who have been involved in a fight so severe that police were called are very likely to have made a low grade point average.

Do you and your girl/boyfriend use alcohol, that is, drink beer, wine, or liquor?

Use of alcohol is correlated with low grades, unless the use is in moderation.

If you see somebody cheating with your boy/girlfriend, will you use deadly force on your friend or both of them?

Saying you would use deadly force against someone cheating with your boy or girl friend, is correlated with making low grades.

Do you think your boy/girlfriend can be of influence in your life regarding decision making?

Not expecting your boy or girl friend to be able to help you make life decisions is correlated with making low grades.

Do you want to influence your friend for your betterment?

Not wanting to influence your friend for your betterment is correlated with low grades.

However, it is likely that many students misread this question to be asking about influencing their friend for the friend's betterment.

Do you feel emotionally attached to your friend?

Not feeling emotionally attached to your boy or girl friend, is correlated with low grades.

Does your friend discuss all his/her problems and issues with you?

Students who made low grades tended to answer no to this question, and students who made high grades tended to answer yes to this question.

Have either of you purchased an engagement ring for the other?

Having bought an engagement ring for your boy or girl friend is correlated with low grade point average.

GPA by Religious Affiliation

It appears that Anglicans (significance = 0.04) and Muslims (Significance = 0.03) make worse grades than average.

The following demographics and survey questions showed no relationship to Grade Point Average.

Gender
Birth Order
Marital Status
Number of Children
Where currently live
Generation of student
Participated in religious activities in past year
Currently participate in religious activities
Religious practice Mediate
Religious practice Deep relaxation
Religious practice Contemplate
Do you and your boy or girl friend attend the same college or university?
Do you plan to marry or engage to your boy or girl friend?
Do you always study together with your boy or girl friend?
If not living together, how many times do you see each other on a daily basis?
How many times do you and your boy/girlfriend call each other on the telephone?
What is your area of study in the areas of science and arts?
Do you or your girlfriend or boyfriend have a baby for someone else?
How often do you text your boy/girlfriend?
How long have you been in this relationship as an intimate one?

KEYWORDS:

Relationship, intimate friend, College/University, senior, acquaintance, stages, Influence, boy/girl, G.P.A, Association, Chi square.

INTRODUCTION

In generic terms, friendship, or relationship is a mutual affection between two or more people (English Dictionary, 2011). An intimate friendship is a stronger form of interpersonal bond, than mere association (Willis, 2011). Social scientists have long been studying friendships, in academic fields, such as criminology, criminal justice, psychology, anthropology philosophy etc. Scholars, such as Brace, Ford, Sparks etc. have proposed theories of friendship which include social exchange theory, equity theory, relational dialectics, and attachment styles. , However, these theories have not been expounded stalwartly and universally. There has not been many researches done efficaciously in these broad social fields on boyfriend/ girlfriend relationships, and their impact on college or university success in the developing countries, except in the present investigation.

There are only a few similar studies in non-adult social psychological researches (Grabmeier, 2004). A world happiness database study, found that people with intimate or close friendships are happier (Wikipedia (2014) "Friendship"), Contrast this conclusion with the observation that some intimate relationships are the cause of stress and unhappiness.

There are notable types of relationships that might vary from one geo-political area to another. The characteristic types of relationships listed herein, include but are not limited to the following: affection, sympathy, honesty, altruism, mutual understanding, compassion, enjoyment of each other's company, trust, the ability to be one self, expression of one's feeling, and mistakes without fear of judgment from the friend. These characteristic types concerning friendship include but are not limited to college or university student contexts. Intimate relationships are sometimes awful or awesome, depending on the racial, cultural or economic stance of the two friends.

A problem of this study is that there is not any practical limit or emotional limit on the types of relationships formed. Individuals holding good relationships are likely to share common backgrounds, the same occupation, common interest, the same culture, and usually similar demographics. If the relationship lacks some or more of the common back grounds, the relationship may be shaky, and may likely result in breakup, and eventually end up in unexpected rebuff, and or discrepancies. One's intimate friend, male/female in a four year college/university is the major focus of this survey research. The research question of this investigation is whether there is an association, between (GPA) grade point average and measures of intimacy among friends. Chi-square analysis is the method used to determine whether such associations exist.

The purpose of this study is to verify, whether or not there are associations between measures of intimate relationships and grade point average of college students from 371 students in Nigeria who were surveyed by the use of questionnaires, using paper- and pencil instruments in the above named country's randomly selected colleges and universities in the year 2013. Friendships grow over time, and by stages, until the two friends become intimate. In this paper I focus on male and female college student's intimate friendships. "Not every friendship or relationship, reaches the intimate stage or best or close friends status because individuals differ, in their backgrounds, such as cultural and racial differences" (Burbach ,2014). Some relationships may start out only as acquaintances, and continue for a longtime before moving to the long-term relationship. Some friendships may move faster than others may, but the speed of friendship development depends on the type of people involved and circumstances such as racial differences, age, cultural, and other various background characteristics. Achievement of intimate friendship requires that each friend devote significant time to build the relationship.

The main purpose of this research is to demonstrate the use of survey research methodology. I analyze a modern generation of young adult male/female students in colleges/ universities in a developing society in Nigeria, where relationships between male and female younger adult students, are monitored by parents or significant others in the family. The purpose is also to garner information that helps individual adults in relationships or who intend to involve themselves in a relationship, so that they know the techniques, of handling friendship.

It is noted by social researchers that various theories have been put in place to account for changes in the levels of relationships, but none of those researchers or theories made use of survey on senior college students in four year colleges or universities in a developing country as did this current research. This is a unique investigation unlike that of the western countries, where relationships are unmonitored by parents or significant others, within the family when one is in college, nor do those theories advance the impact of an intimate relationships on the college grade point average, using survey method of analysis. Currently a clear hierarchy of explanatory theories is in vogue. Some theories are always treated as master explanatory theories. Those theories are value laden as opposed to value free, and are always considered as superior by some researchers and scholars. I admit that I myself have not been able to reach the level of value free research.

An acquaintance is an occasional relationship between two persons, or one who knows another person in passing, which involves interaction occasionally or just on a regular basis. However, the person who you see occasionally may regard you as a friend, and an acquaintance may become a friend, when you see each other regularly (Burbach, 2014).

Many theoretical and practical consequences flow from this study. In a glance at its theoretical and practical consequences, one can identify several points of departure. This research will help show how relationship levels can be useful to explain research results. In addition, this research illustrates a comparative study in human relationship theory. This research shows the study of "Intimate relationships." Other levels of relationships (see above) could be of importance as well. Similar research could fill a glaring gap in the academic journals, in relationship theory, and other related social theories as well. Mille, Miller, and Perlman (1991) support the contemplation in their book "Intimate Relationships", published in 1991:

Ancient philosophers considered the ideas of marital satisfaction, faithfulness, beauty, and jealously. However, the concepts and the explanations they gave were often inaccurate or misleading. Over 2,300 years ago, Aristotle wrote about interpersonal relationships. He wrote: "A person is a friend to another, if he is friendly to the other, and the other is friendly to him in return" (Aristotle, 330 BC, trans. 1991, .72-73). Aristotle believed that by nature humans are social beings. Aristotle, 330BC, gave an opinion that might be fallacious. However, I accept his suggestions, but not with absolute certainty. Relationships, according to Aristotle, may be based on three different ideas: utility, pleasure, and virtue.

The current research investigates whether people are attracted to relationships that provide utility because of the assistance and sense of belonging that they provide. Relationships based on utility, and pleasure, are attractive because of the feelings of pleasantness when the parties are together. (Aristotle 330 B.C.)However, relationships based on utility and pleasures have been strongly debated to be short-lived, if the benefits provided by one of the partners were not reciprocated. It was also noted that relationships based on virtue are always built on an attraction to the other virtuous character (Wiki/ intimate relationship retrieved 2014).

Aristotle put up preposition, in which he argued or contended that relationships based on virtue would be the longest lasting, and that virtue-based relationships were the only type of relationships in which each partner was liked for himself or herself. (Aristotle, 330 B.C) Although Aristotle, like many ancient philosophers, made many statements about relationships he did not use scientific methods, and therefore he could not conclude that his thoughts and ideas were correct (Wiki/ Intimate relationship retrieved 2014).

The philosophical analysis used by Aristotle dominated the analysis of intimate relationships. The present investigation does not argue on why people had or have relationships, but shows the outcomes of intimate relationships for Senior students in four year colleges in Nigeria, a developing country in Africa, where relationships among young adults are monitored by parents or significant others. This is the major uniqueness of the current research. Another aspect of the current research is that it is a precedent for similar comparison studies.

THEORECTICAL AND CONCEPTUAL FRAMEWORK

A theoretical framework is a compilation of interrelated concepts. Theoretical frameworks may guides individuals in doing research; or determine the type of measurement or statistical apparatus the researcher plans to use. Online friends through email or, Facebook, Twitter etc. could fuel one's life in many ways, and may lead to closer relationships (Burbach, 2014). Friends interact with each other in the internet, where their faces, page, and forums are available 24 hours around the clock. , At any time, online friends can enhance one's life. Whoever you have a relationship with, or have spent time with, and bonded with, may be considered a friend, but not necessarily an intimate friend. One may start up as good friends with someone, and become intimate friends, or drift apart or become only occasional friends.

Friendships are directional. One direction is your befriending someone. The other direction is when another befriends you. Intimate friendships in one direction may be slightly different than in the other direction. In addition, the two friendship directions may be at different levels.

Thus, felt relationships are not necessarily mutual. A close friend is one you consider as a part of your inner circle. They know the style of life of each other. One sees a good friend often and talks with him or her often (Burbach, 2014)

.Burbach (2014) maintains the idea that best friends are close friends. They are considered as friends that one spends a great deal of time with, and cares for. Close friends are also the ones one can spend money on, or rescue, if he or she is in trouble, or gets hurt.

Again, being a close friend is like being a member of the family. Close friends share secrets, and they care for each other. They feel secure, when they are together. Close friends are always happy when they are together. They are often sexually attracted to each other. They always feel comfortable when they are together. They can imitate or copy each other's behavior, Burbach 2014; Rhale, 2004; Kakabadse, Kakabadse, 2004; Daniel, 2008; Moore, 1985). They can share the same values. Sometimes they share despair, because of circumstances, such as the process of breaking up the relationship, economic hardships, or lack of interaction, or communication. Distant relationships are all problematic, but the level of relationship depends on the level of understanding of the two friends (Fuller, 2011; Costello, 2009).

INTIMATE FRIENDSHIP

An intimate relationship or friendship is a close relationship, which is always interpersonal, and sometimes involves physical and emotional intimacy. The physical aspect of intimate friendship is characterized by romantic passionate attachment, and sexual activity. Sometimes it results in mistresship or marriage (Daniel, 2008;

Miller, Rowland and Perlman, (eds Daniel, 2008). The term intimate friend almost always implies the inclusion of sexual relationship, and sometimes used as an euphemism for friendship which is strictly or specifically sexual (Daniel, 2008).

The Concept of Intimate Friendship

Pelman, argues that intimate friendships play a central role in the overall human circumstances and experiences. Pelman, continues to argue that humans have a general desire to belong and to be loved, which is usually satisfied by intimate relationships. The relationships in the current investigation involve feelings of liking or loving one another, romance, physical or sexual attraction, sexual relationships, or emotional and personal support. The concept of Intimate friendships includes strong emotional attachments within a social network. (Pelman, 2007). The current research does not imply the concept of social network for people to form strong emotional attachment, because this research is specifically the involvement of only two people, male/female while in college or university to determine how that relationship affects their college grade point average.

A person's feeling of being in a close personal association and belonging together is referred to as intimacy. (Dalton, 1959). Dalton maintains that close affective connection with another, as a result of a bond formed through knowledge and experience of the other, is always an effective relationship. Genuine intimacy in human relationships, as in the current investigation, requires dialogue, transparency vulnerability, and reciprocity.

The verb "intimate," as used by Dalton (1959) means "to state or make known". The activity of intimating (making known) underpins the meanings of "intimate" when used as an adjective. The noun "intimate" means a person with whom one has an intimate relationship. Dalton drew information and expounded on how anthropologists and ethnographics access "inside information" from within a particular cultural setting by establishing networks of intimates capable and willing to provide information unobtainable through formal channels. Dalton also contends that the adjective "intimate" indicates detailed knowledge of a thing or person. He has "an intimate knowledge of engineering". Those two have an "intimate relationship".

In the current investigation and generally in human relationships, the meaning and level of intimacy varies within and between relationships. In anthropological research, intimacy is considered to be the product of a successful seduction, a process of rapport building that enables parties to confidently disclose previously hidden thoughts and feelings. Intimate conversations become the basis for "confidences" (secret knowledge), that bind people together. To sustain intimacy for any length of time requires well-developed emotional and interpersonal awareness. Intimacy requires an ability to be both separate and together by participants in an intimate relationship (Dalton, 1959). Murray Bowen called this "self-differentiation" that results in a connection with an emotional range involving both robust conflict, and intense loyalty. Lacking the ability, (free encyclopedia, and 2014) to differentiate oneself from the other is a form of symbiosis. Symbiosis is different from intimacy, even if feelings of closeness are similar.

From a center of self-knowledge and self-differentiation, intimate behavior joins family members and close friends as well as those in love. It evolves through reciprocal self-disclosure and candor

(Dalton, 1959). Dalton argues that poor skills in developing intimacy can lead to getting too close too quickly; struggling to find the boundary and to sustain connection; being perceived as not a good friend, rejecting self-disclosure or even rejecting friendships and friends. Intimacy problems are found in adults who have difficulty in forming and maintaining intimate relationships. Individuals according to Dalton often experience the human limitations of their partners, and develop a fear of adverse consequences of disrupted intimate relationships, Ridley, (2010) contends that several studies show that fear of intimacy is sometimes negatively correlated to being comfortable with emotional closeness and with relationship satisfaction, and also sometimes positively related to trait anxiety and feelings of loneliness.

Forms of intimacy

It is noteworthy to mention that scholars such as distinguish between four different forms of intimacy: physical, emotional, cognitive, and experiential intimacy (Kakabadse, A., Kakabadse, N., 2004). These scholars argue that physical intimacy is sensual proximity or touching, examples include being inside someone's personal space, holding hands, hugging, kissing, caressing, and other sexual activity. They maintain that emotional intimacy, particularly in sexual relationships, typically develops after a certain level of trust has been established. The emotional connection of "falling in love", however, has both a biochemical dimension, driven through reactions in the body stimulated by sexual attraction, and a social dimension driven by "talk" that follows from physical closeness or sexual union (Ridley-Duff, 2010). Cognitive or intellectual intimacy takes place when two people exchange thoughts, share ideas and enjoy similarities and differences between their opinions (Ridley-Duff, 2010). If they can do this in an open and comfortable way, they can become quite intimate in an intellectual arena. Experiential intimacy is expected when two people can get together to actively involve themselves with each other, probably saying very little to each other, not sharing any thoughts or many feelings, but being involved in mutual activities with one another. (Fuller, 2011), "Imagine observing two house painters whose brushstrokes seemed to be playing out a duet on the side of the house". The imaginary two painters may be shocked to think that they were engaged in an intimate activity with each other, however from an experiential point of view, they would be intimately involved.

It is worth distinguishing intimate (communal) relationships from strategic (exchange) relationships (Daniel, 2008). Physical intimacy, according to Daniel, occurs in strategic relationships, but it is governed by a higher-order strategy of one of the couple, of which the other person may not be aware. One example is getting close to someone in order to get something from him or her or give them something (Daniel, 2008). That offer might not be made so freely, if it did not appear to be an intimate exchange and if the ultimate goal had been visible at the outset. Mills and Clark (1982) found that strategic (exchange) relationships are fragile and easily break down when there is any level of disagreement. Emotionally intimate (communal) relationships are much more robust and can survive considerable (and even ongoing) disagreements. (Wiki/intimate relationship, retrieved 2014)

Physical and emotional intimacy

"Love" according to Hatfield (1993) is an important factor in physical and emotional intimate relationships. He argues that love is qualitatively different from liking, and the difference is not merely in the presence or absence of sexual attraction. Hatfield argues that there are two types of love in a relationship; "passionate love" and "companionate love." "Companionate love involves diminished feelings of attachment, an authentic and enduring bond, a sense of mutual commitment, the profound feeling of mutual caring, feeling proud of mate's accomplishment and the satisfaction that comes from sharing goals and perspective". In contrast according to Hatfield (1993), passionate love is marked by infatuation, intense preoccupation with the partner, throes of ecstasy, and feelings of exhilaration that come from being reunited with the partner.

Two people who are in an intimate relationship with one another, according to Hatfield, are often called a couple, especially, if the members of that couple have placed some degree of permanency onto their relationship, Social scholars affirm that under these conditions, permanent relationship becomes the status quo. These couples often provide the emotional security that is necessary for them to accomplish other tasks, particular forms of labor or work. Whether or not the couple's relationship would affect the college/

university success as measured by grade point average is one of the research questions of the current investigation.

Psychology and sociology began to emerge in the late 19th century (Wiki/intimate relationship, 2014). During this time, theorists often included study of relationships in their research. They began to develop new theoretical foundations for the analysis of intimate relationships.

Freud wrote about parent-child relationships, and their effect on personality development. Freud's analysis proposed that people's childhood experiences transform relationships by means of feelings and expectations. Sigmund Freud also founded the idea that individuals usually seek out marital partners who are similar to that of their opposite-sex parents. (Wiki/intimate relationship, retrieved 2014) Khaleque, 2004; and Kakabads, and Kakabads, 2004)

In 1891, William James, in the "Principles of Psychology", wrote that a person's self-concept is defined by the relationships endured with others (Wiki/intimate relationships, retrieved 2014). In 1897, Durkheim's interest in social organization led to the examination of social isolation and alienation (Kakabads and Kakabads, 2004). In this influential study of intimate relationships, Durkheim argues that being socially isolated was a key antecedent of suicide. This focus is on the darker side of relationships, and the negative consequences attributed to social isolation were what Durkheim labeled as anomie. , In the 1950s, Simmel examined unique properties of dyads, or partnership with two people (Miller, Rowland & Perlman, Daniel ,2008). Simmel suggested that dyads require consent and engagement of only one partner. Although these theorists sought support for their theories, their primary contributions to the study of intimate relationships were conceptual and not empirically grounded. The current investigation is, empirical and thus is not limited to the conceptualization mode of analysis.

The use of empirical investigations in 1898 was a major revolution in social analysis. A study conducted by Monroe, examined the traits and habits of children in selecting a friend. Some of the attributes included in that study were kindness, cheerfulness and honesty. Monroe asked 2336 children aged 7 to 16 to identify "what kind of chum do you like best?" The results show that children preferred a friend that was their own age, of the same gender, of the same body size, a friend with light features (hair and eyes), did not involve themselves in conflict, someone that was kind to animals, and humans, and finally that they were honest. The two characteristics that children reported as least important included wealth and religion. This study by Monroe, is a foundation for examining intimate friendship in college, and how the intimacy impacts on their college success as measured by grade point average.

This study by Monroe was the first to mark the significant shift in the study of intimate relationships from analysis that was primarily philosophical to those with empirical validity. Empirical studies are said to be the beginning of relationship science. There were limited empirical studies done on children's friendships, courtships and marriages, and families in the 1930s, but few relationship studies were conducted before or during World War II. Intimate relationships did not become a broad focus of research again until the 1960s and 1970s when there were a vast amount of relationship studies being published (Wikipedia (2014) " Intimate Relationship ")

It was in the 1960's and 1970's that publications reflected an important shift on empirical research in the field of social psychology. Those publications really influenced further research on intimate relationships. The 1960s was also a time when there was a shift in methods within the social and psychological discipline (Dalton 1959). Just as in the current investigation, participants consisted of almost all college students. Experimental methods were used in research that was conducted in laboratories. At that time the experimental method was the dominant methodology in social psychology itself (Dalton 1959).

Experimental manipulation within the research of intimate relationships demonstrated that relationships could be studied scientifically (Daniel 2008). This shift in methods brought relationship science to attention of scholars in other disciplines. It has resulted in the study of intimate relationships being an international multidiscipline (Daniel 2008).

Another evidence of growing interest in study of interpersonal relationships is the organized conferences on the topic. In the early 1980s the first conference of the International Network of Personal Relationships (INPR) was held. Approximately 300 researchers from all over the world attended the conference. In March 1984, the first journal of Social and Personal Relationships was published (Wiki/intimate relationship,2014). In the early 1990s the INPR split off into two groups; in April 2004 the two organizations rejoined and became the International Association for Relationship Research (IARR) (Burbach 2014).

According to Donald Nathanson (1987), a psychiatrist, intimate relationship between two individuals is best when the couple agrees to maximize positive affect, minimize negative affect and express affection freely.

Current studies

Today, in the 21st century, the study of intimate relationships (relationship science) uses participants from diverse groups. Researchers examine a wide variety of topics, including family relations, friendships, and romantic relationships. John Gottman and his colleagues invite married couples into a pleasant setting, in which they revisit the disagreement that caused their last argument. The participants are aware that they are being videotaped, but they soon become so absorbed in their own interaction that they forget they are being recorded. With the second-by-second analysis of observable reactions as well as emotional ones, Gottman is able to predict with 93% accuracy the fate of the couples' relationship (Wikipedia (2014) " Intimate Relationship ").

Terri Orbuch and Joseph Veroff conduct another current area of research into intimate relationships (Miller, Rowland & Perlman, Daniel, 2008) They monitor newlywed couples using self-reports over a long period (a longitudinal study). Participants are required to provide extensive reports about the natures and the statuses of their relationships. Although many of the marriages have ended since the beginning of the study, this type of relationship study allows researchers to track marriages from start to finish by conducting follow-up interviews with the participants in order to determine which factors are associated with marriages that last and which with those that do not. Though the field of intimate relationship in the social sciences is still relatively young, (Wiki/ Intimate relationship, retrieved 2014) Researchers from different disciplines continue to broaden the field.

Evidence drawn from Lowe and Scoglio (2012) also points to the role of a number of contextual factors that can affect intimate relationships. In a recent study on the impact of Hurricane Katrina on marital and partner relationships, researchers found that while many people reported negative changes in their relationships, a number also experienced positive changes. Abundantly and specifically, the advent of Hurricane Katrina led to a number of environmental stressors (e.g., unemployment, prolonged separation) that negatively impacted intimate relationships.. However, some couples' relationships grew stronger as a result of new employment opportunities, a greater sense of perspective, and higher levels of communication and support. Based on this, environmental factors are also understood to contribute heavily to the strength of intimate relationships. (Wiki/ intimate relationships, retrieved 2014)

One study by Reczek (2011); and Fuller, (2011) suggests that married straight couples and cohabiting gay and lesbian couples in long-term intimate relationships may pick up each other's unhealthy habits. The study reports three distinct findings showing how unhealthy habits are promoted in long-term, intimate relationships:

[1] through the direct bad influence of one partner, [2] through synchronicity of health habits, and [3] through the notion of personal responsibility. (Wiki/ Intimate relationship, retrieved 2014)

Anthropologist Robin Dunbar postulated in 1992 that the average number of people that one could maintain a "stable social relationship" with ranged from 100 to 230, with a conventional average of 150. His definition of a network is one in which "an individual knows who each person is and how each person relates to every other person." But Dunbar proposed this number in 1992, before the advent of Twitter, Facebook, LinkedIn, and a deluge of other social media applications which bring people closer together than ever before. Could it be that Dunbar was right in 1992, but wrong in 2013? Despite the increased access to people via social media, it appears that Dunbar's number still holds true. Although individuals today may contact a vast array of people scattered across the globe, researchers have thus far been unable to disprove 150 as an average maximum threshold of stable social relationships. Messaging with one's "friends" on Facebook has been shown to provoke a different biological response than talking with one's friend's in-person, (Dunbar, 1992).

In 1992, Dunbar published a research paper in the Journal of Human Evolution entitled "Neocortex size as a constraint on group size in primates". In his paper, he proposed that the size of the human neocortex would predict the number of other people with whom individuals could maintain a "stable social relationship" The neocortex is responsible for a variety of higher level human functions including sensory perception, conscious thought and language. It is because of its importance in communication, that Dunbar conducted a regression of the ratio of the size of the neocortex to the hindbrain against the mean number of stable social relationships held by primates of a particular genus. Conducting this regression over 38 distinct primate genera, he found a statistically significant relationship.

When applied to humans, Dunbar predicted, with a 95% confidence interval the mean to be 148, which is typically rounded to 150 for its aesthetic roundness. The probable range of number of friends is between 100 and 230. Dunbar then searched through previous eras for historical justification of his number. He found supporting examples of 150 in a wide variety of contexts in anthropological literature. Thus, in 1992, Dunbar's number was born, (Modern-Day Dunbar's number-network 209 wiki, 2004)

Dunbar (1992) notes that 150 is just an average, with some people gravitating towards fewer or more friends. Faith in Dunbar's number has led to variety of profound applications. For example, Bill Gore, leader and founder of the company Gore-Tex, employed Dunbar's number as a principle to organize his business. As Gore-Tex company grew over time, he realized it was becoming more and more difficult to maintain a close, personal connection with everyone. To preserve the close-knit community feel that would spur employees to help each other out, he capped the maximum number of employees in each factory to 150.

 It was noted by scholars that Dunbar's number flies in the face of networks like Facebook, where the average US user has 303 friends. , Some social media have supported and even built themselves around Dunbar's number. Path, for instance, explicitly caps users' total allowed number of friends at 150. Their rationale is to help users maintain relationships with "people who matter most in your life"

The Dunbar hypothesis (1992) was put in practice by the military, which organizes itself around Dunbar,'s number as well. Perhaps no other environment demands as much team cohesion and morale as the military. In life-or-death situations, gut instincts about whether ones platoon-mate would cover your back will have a major impact on the effectiveness of one's team. Military companies, the building blocks of a larger battalion do, range in size from 80-225 soldiers, of course a very similar range to Dunbar's estimated range of 100-230. Military analysts responsible for allocating personnel make company sizes according to Dunbar's number. (Modern Day Dunbar number network/ The Dunbar's hypothesis does not apply to the current investigation because my unit of analysis is one intimate relationship between two people.

Conger, J.J and Galambos, N (1997) contributed immensely to the field of developmental psychology, by utilizing typical sequences within an individual's emotional development. They emphasized that pair bonding (friendships) come after parental bonding and that human development involves reasonable foresight. They argued that in the intervening period between the end of early childhood and the onset of full adulthood, friendships are often the most important relationships in the emotional life of adolescent, and often more intense than relationships later in life (Conger and Galambos, 1997).

Homosexuality and Friendship

I suggest, based on my observation in the U.S, that homophobia has been, and is still at the decrease in the western world. The actual involvement in homosexuality is surprisingly in the increase, due to its legality. In Nigeria and in many developing African/ Middle or near East countries, homosexuality is considered a criminal act and sin, at the same time. There the experience of being homosexual could be homoerotic, or traumatic, and could limit the potential for "same sex friendships," (Jnanavira 2013). In the current investigation, because the respondents live in Nigeria, I presume that all respondents are heterosexual.

CULTURE: ITS IMPACTS ON RELATIONSHIPS IN SOME COUNTRIES

Friendship was a much-discussed topic among Ancient Greek moral philosophers. Plato, Aristotle, and the Stoics discussed this topic, "Friendship". In Ancient Greece, a friend was one you treated as you would treat yourself.

However, in the modern Greek era, the topic of "friendship" was less often discussed until the reemergence of conceptualists and the feminist approaches to the ethical world.

In East Asia friendship, is formed during youth. In the East Asians view, friendship requires fidelity. In East Asia, fair weather friends are not considered friends. Only close friends are acknowledged to be friends. Friendships in this region start early in life, and can grow or wax stronger, through contact over years of schooling, and or working. They usually have a close "tight knit" relationships unlike friendships in the United States (Said, 1979).

In the western countries culture, people regard multiple friends as their "best friends." Being one's friend in East Asian culture is considered an honor and privilege to each other. In China, the view is that good friendships require continual enhancement. (Said, 1979). Said (1979) notes that relationships between friends in the East, and Central Asian culture holds a tight bond that is not easily broken. However, if one of the two friends moves to another geopolitical region or another country, the bond would be broken. (Said, 1979).

The present investigation emphasizes an intimate relationship of college and university students. It examines the impacts of such senior student's intimate relationships on their college or university success as measured by grade point average.

Germans' friendship (Nees 2000) might surprise you because of their nature and circumstances surrounding the country, such as law, policies and weather conditions. Germans, in general, always have few friends, but their friendships usually last for life time (Nees, 2000).

In Germany, friendship provides a substantive amount of commitment and support, (Nees, 2000). Germans may seem to appear unsympathetic or aloof to people from other countries, because they are always cautious, as to keep their distance not to develop intimate relationship with new or unfamiliar individuals around them. Nees continues to emphasize that Germans do draw distinct boundaries among their few friends, associates, coworkers, neighbors and students. Examples of such boundaries are: Are they foreigners; Are they German; Are they familiar?

In Islamic countries, the concept of friendship (2012), is that friendship is companionship or "*ashab.*" The concept of friendship is taken very seriously with several attributes. You would probably ask if your friend is righteous or "*saalih.*" Righteous friends can appropriately draw a line between uprightness, rule, habit or evil. Non Islamic people need to be aware of the Islamic requirements of friendship if they are to make friends with people of the Islamic religion. Forgiveness of mistakes and loyalty between friends is constantly taken into consideration in the development of friendship. Bringing "love for the sake of Allah," is considered to be the most intimate relationship and of the highest definitional awesomeness between two human friends in the Islamic religious culture (Nees, 2012).

Middle East or Near East people believe, according to (Radwan 2014), that friendship is a stalwart phenomenon that demands unity or oneness to avoid silent betrayal of trust. Radwan contends that, in the near east, friendships are between two people who respect each other's wellbeing, regardless of all odds or shortcomings of each other. A friend may commit himself to making personal sacrifices to assist a fellow friend, putting himself in the same shoes and without considering the experience to be an imposition on him. (Radwan, 2014). Many Arabians, contends Radwan (2014), do perceive friendship very seriously. The choice of friends may depend on social influence and the nature of the potential friend's character'.

Russian friendships (Babaeva, 2010) are framed by the qualities of Modern Russia in the soviet times. Hardship in the then (USSR) forced the many Russians to create relationships with people in many businesses, in order to survive hardship or survive the scarcity they were into at the time. Babaeva, notes that the Russians needed the medical care they could not easily afford. Many solved their problem by making friends with hospital employees in order to obtain medical attention. Such practices notes Babaeva (2010) led to a community spirit and interpersonal connections. Most of these practical friendships that developed in Russia remain till the present day. Inefficiencies in the part of the Russian government made it easier for Russians to rely on their friends, and family than in any company or business. These traditional types of relationship in Russia, then and now, are valued greatly (Babaeva 2010).

There were various conditions in the soviet Period that made it necessary for Russians to form friendships. In Russia, at that time, to confide in another opened the risk of being reported to the state especially for different opinions about Russia.   German people in soviet communities had very few friends, but were extremely close with those they had. The same mode of behavior on friendships making still tends to exist in the present day Russia.

Stout (2010) observed that there are many types of relationships that are considered friendships in the United States of America. In the U.S., from the time children enter elementary school friendships have started to develop. In the U.S., teachers and adults call their peers "friends," but "boy friends" and "girl friends" are close friends or intimate friends. In the U.S. adults teach most children, in the classrooms and in the social settings, on how to behave with their friends.

The way adults in the U.S. openly emphasize friendship, led many adults to designate a "best friend," with whom they are especially intimate. (Stout, 2010). This designation or specification of friends that are close has created a lot of problems in the U.S society.

Most U.S girls believe that boy/friends will be their husbands, whereas, based on my observations and experiences, such relationships rarely result in marriage. It has caused U.A. citizens, mostly Blacks, continuously to produce illegitimate children, which creates problems of child support. When the dad runs away, or is unable to provide that child support, the mother and grandparents must provide for it. These fathers can leave to another city to do the same thing to other girls. The girls need to learn how to not treat their boyfriends as potential husbands (Liz Lampkin,May 19, 2012). A single girl in the U.S. can have five to six children from several men that are unmarried to them. The males tend to be high school dropouts (holigans) or members of street gangs who could not afford any money to pay child supports. The girls call police for those who fail to pay child support. The next thing after the police arrests would be to charge such young boys as violators of child support and thence to the special family court, and to prison. Most of the college level dropouts are put in prisons for failure to pay child supports. The girls with five to six children get low-cost housing for the poor, and never wanted to have jobs or get education, but depend on food-stamps for survival, while the males spend all their lives in prisons and on the street as homeless or street gangs.

This view of close friendship, according to Stout (2010), in the U.S. has led many Adolescents to risk killing their girlfriend, when the girl become close or intimate but wants to leave boyfriend. Thousands of girls in the U.S. lose their lives by their so called boyfriends who are always the poor ones in the society. The problem again in the U.S. is designating an open emphasis on boyfriend/ girlfriend. Nevertheless, it is a culture that continues forever, specifically within the underclass, poor blacks. They bluntly refuse to accept good advices, because everybody within the lower classes feels that they are grown and free to act anyhow. They accept no guidelines for behavior or for where to go or for what types of friend to have. They act on their own, and eventually usually make mistakes of choices of friends.

U.S. friends tend to be people whom they encounter frequently, and are similar to themselves in demographics, attitude, and social level (Stout 2010). Contrary to many other cultures that value deep trust and meaning in their friendships, U.S. citizens use the word "friend" to describe people they meet often who have qualities similar to themselves (Stout, 2010). U.S. men have less deep and meaningful friendships with other men (Stout, 2010). Many men and women in the U.S. have similar definitions of intimacy, but women in the U.S are more likely to practice intimacy in friendships (Wikipedia (2014) "Friendship"). U.S. adults lose touch with many friends for no explicit reasons for doing so. This is specifically true of women. Having intimate or romantic relationships with young women in the U.S. would not prevent them from leaving you anytime, only because they met a new friend. A study published in American Sociological Review indicates that, since 1985, U.S. citizens suffer losses in the quality and quantity of close friends (Kornblum, 2006 and McPherson; and Smith-lovin, 2006). The study made it clear that one quarter of all Americans have no close confidants, and that the average total number of confidants per person has dropped from four to two.

All these countries and cultures in regard to friendship discussed above differ in large extent from the present investigation. The present investigation is a survey research, conducted in a few selected colleges/ universities in Nigeria, where intimate relations are monitored by parents, or significant others in the family. Chi-square analysis methods were used. Chi-square test enables me to compare the observed and the expected frequencies objectively, since it is not possible to tell just by looking at them whether they are different enough to be considered statistically significant.

METHODS, DATA COLLECTION AND HYPOTHESES

This investigation uses a survey research methodology. A Survey is a non-experimental descriptive research method. It is a method of collecting data on phenomena, which is not directly observed, such as opinion from intimate friendship or relationships such as in the present investigation. Surveys are mostly used in the information Sciences to assess and document the attitudes and characteristics of a group, and the impacts that the group has on particular or specific individuals within the group. Researchers use surveys to characterize a sample of a population and then infer those characteristics to the larger population. It is necessary that the sample size be sufficiently large, and that individuals in the associated larger population have the same average exogenous characteristics as in the sample. In the current investigation I randomly selected a few four year colleges and universities, collected information from senior students vis a vis male/female intimate relationships, and how that relationship impacted on their college or university success as measured by grade point average. Questionnaires were distributed to the respondent students in the classrooms. The students utilized paper and pencil instruments to answer the questions. The questions were simple open-ended questions. I believes that when the phenomena that I want to collect data on is not observable, the simplest method of collecting data from respondents would be the survey method. The current investigation, which solicits opinions from two intimate friends concerning their relationship, uses survey method for that reason.

I used Chi Square statistics to evaluate the survey results. The questions they answered were "forced choice" questions. However, in practice, it was not possible to force a choice because respondents had the option of not answering, or writing in a different answer. This sometimes made it somewhat difficult, but not impossible, to interpret the chi square statistics.

I use a cross-sectional survey to gather information on a population of students mentioned above, at a single point in time. The cross sectional survey questionnaire tries to determine the relationship between two characteristics, such as boyfriend/ girlfriend intimate relationships and how it affects the students (GPA) great point average. I use Chi-Square test to determine whether the observed frequencies are significantly different from expected frequencies. For example, I calculated the expected frequencies from different senior students in four year selected colleges or universities in Nigeria, who were involved in intimate relationships. Then I use the Chi-Square test to compare the observed and the expected frequencies and determine whether there is a statistical difference between boyfriend/girlfriend intimate relationship characteristics and grade point average.

My Null hypothesis Ho is that, for each cross tabulation of a characteristic of an intimate relationship with grade point average, there is no significant difference between observed and the expected frequencies. My alternative hypothesis H1 is that, for each cross tabulation of a characteristic of an intimate relationship with grade point average, there is a significant difference between observed and expected frequencies. Based on the outcome of the Chi-Square test, the I would either reject or fail to reject the Null hypothesis.

Results

age
[18,25] year old students did better than average. Significance number was 0.089.
[26,35] year old students did worse than average. Significance number was 0.002.
[36,45] year old students did about average. Significance number was 0.257.

Table 1 GPA by Age

Joint Frequency	Total	[18,25]	[26,35]	[36,45]	[46,55]	[56,above]	NA
Total	371	248	100	17	2	1	3
[0,1.5]	11	4	5	2	0	0	0
[1.6,2.4]	42	15	23	3	1	0	0
[2.5,3.49]	174	116	49	7	0	1	1
[3.5,4.49]	91	70	16	5	0	0	0
[4.5,5]	13	9	2	0	0	0	2
NA	40	34	5	0	1	0	0
Significance	0.00	0.09	0.002	0.26	0.32	0.98	0.00

Gender

Average male student GPA is no better or worse than GPA of average female.
Significance scores for Males (0.595) and Females (0.675) confirm that there is no association between gender and GPA.

Table 2 GPA by Gender

Joint Frequency	Total	Male	Female	NA
Total	371	164	205	2
[0,1.5	11	4	7	0
[1.6,2.4]	42	19	22	1
[2.5,3.49]	174	89	84	1
[3.5,4.49]	91	33	58	0
[4.5,5]	13	6	7	0
NA	40	13	27	0
Significance	0.84	0.60	0.68	0.75

Birth Order

None of the significances for birth order were less than 0.1. Thus I conclude that there is no significant association between birth order and Grade point average.

Table 3 GPA by Birth Order

Joint Frequency	Total	First Born	Middle Born	Last Born	NA
Total	371	78	193	85	15
[0,1.5]	11	2	4	4	1
[1.6,2.4]	42	11	18	11	2
[2.5,3.49]	174	36	88	44	6
[3.5,4.49]	91	14	60	16	1
[4.5,5]	13	4	6	2	1
NA	40	11	17	8	4
Significance	0.77	0.76	0.49	0.80	0.34

Marital Status

Overall, there is not an association between marital status and grade point average. The significance numbers for Separated, Divorced, and Widowed are ignored because of the small number of respondents in those groups.

Table 4 GPA by Marital Status

Joint Frequency	Total	Single	Married	Separated	Divorced	Widowed
Total	371	302	57	8	1	3
[0,1.5]	11	5	5	0	1	0
[1.6,2.4]	42	30	5	5	0	2
[2.5,3.49]	174	144	27	2	0	1
[3.5,4.49]	91	78	12	1	0	0
[4.5,5]	13	12	1	0	0	0
NA	40	33	7	0	0	0
Significance	NA	0.75	0.26	NA	NA	NA

Number of Children

None of the significances for number of children was < 0.1. There is not a significant association between number of children and grade point average.

The overall significance number of 0.00 for the table as a whole is explained by the association between grade point average of [1.6, 2.4] with this **number of children** question not being answered. Probably most of the students who did not answer this question had no children.

It would have been better to have added **"no children"** as a possible answer choice.

Then I would have had confirmation for in what way not having any children at all would impact GPA.

Table 5 GPA by Number of Children

Joint Frequency	Total	[1,3]	[4,6]	[6,above]	NA	None
Total	371	69	16	2	229	55
[0,1.5]	11	4	1	0	4	2
[1.6,2.4]	42	13	3	1	15	10
[2.5,3.49]	174	27	9	1	119	18
[3.5,4.49]	91	15	3	0	56	17
[4.5,5]	13	3	0	0	9	1
NA	40	7	0	0	26	7
Significance	NA	0.16	0.38	0.48	0.13	0.18

Currently live

There is not any significant association of where the student currently lives with grade point average.

Table 6 GPA by Currently live

Joint Frequency	Total	In the dormitory	At home with one and or both parents	At home with relatives other than parents	In own apartment	With my boy/girl friend	NA
Total	371	68	71	35	170	18	9
[0,1.5]	11	4	1	3	3	0	0
[1.6,2.4]	42	13	7	6	12	3	1
[2.5,3.49]	174	33	23	16	87	11	4
[3.5,4.49]	91	10	26	5	43	3	4
[4.5,5]	13	1	2	3	7	0	0
NA	40	7	12	2	18	1	0
Significance	0.29	0.17	0.10	0.14	0.62	0.77	0.81

Religious Affiliation

Anglicans (significance = 0.04) and Muslims (Significance = 0.03) have lower grades than the average of the other religious groups.

Table 7 GPA by Religious Affiliation

Joint

Freq	Total	Baptist	Methodist	Catholic	Anglican	Muslim	Other	NA
Total	371	22	27	163	66	11	71	11
[0,1.5]	11	0	0	4	3	1	3	0
[1.6,2.4]	42	2	4	14	14	4	4	0
[2.5,3.49]	174	10	18	72	21	2	45	6
[3.5,4.49]	91	5	3	45	21	1	13	3
[4.5,5]	13	2	0	10	0	0	1	0
NA	40	3	2	18	7	3	5	2
Signif	0.10	0.82	0.36	0.50	0.04	0.03	0.15	0.85

Generation of student

There is no association between generation of student and grade point average.

Table 8 GPA by Generation of student

Joint Frequency	Total	1st generation	2nd generation	3rd generation	NA
Total	371	67	82	144	78
[0,1.5]	11	0	4	6	1
[1.6,2.4]	42	12	9	17	4
[2.5,3.49]	174	33	42	58	41
[3.5,4.49]	91	14	20	41	16
[4.5,5]	13	2	3	7	1
NA	40	6	4	15	15
Significance	NA	0.26	0.41	0.44	NA

Adult child of an alcoholic?

Children of alcoholics tend to make lower grades than do others. Significance = 0.02. However, many children of alcoholics do make average or better grades.

Table 9 GPA by Adult child of an alcoholic?

Joint Frequency	Total	Yes	No	NA
Total	371	21	336	14
[0,1.5]	11	3	8	0
[1.6,2.4]	42	3	39	0
[2.5,3.49]	174	11	155	8
[3.5,4.49]	91	2	86	3
[4.5,5]	13	2	11	0
NA	40	0	37	3
Significance	0.29	0.02	0.99	0.63

Participate in religious activities in past year

There is no significant association between frequency of religious activities and grade point average.
The number of students who attended religious services for only a few times last year, and also made low grades, is significant.
However, the number of students who attend religious services for only a few times last year, and make average or high grades, is not significant.

Table 10 GPA by Participate in religious activities in past year

Joint Frequency	Total	Daily	A few times a week	Once a week	Afew times a month	A few times a year	Never	NA
Total	371	98	167	64	20	16	0	6
[0,1.5]	11	1	2	4	1	3	0	0
[1.6,2.4]	42	9	15	11	1	6	0	0
[2.5,3.49]	174	45	81	26	13	5	0	4
[3.5,4.49]	91	29	42	15	4	1	0	0
[4.5,5]	13	6	6	1	0	0	0	0
NA	40	8	21	7	1	1	0	2
Significance	0.05	0.51	0.79	0.48	0.69	0.00	NA	0.44

Currently participate in religious activities

The association between "Currently participate in religious activities" and grade point average is very similar to the association between "Participate in religious activities last year" and Grade Point Average. There is no significant association between Currently participate in religious activities and grade point average.

Table 11 GPA by Currently participate in religious activities

Joint Freq	Total	Daily	A few times a week	Once a week	A few times a month	A few times a year	Never	NA
Total	371	103	156	80	12	9	5	6
[0,1.5]	11	2	1	4	0	3	1	0
[1.6,2.4]	42	14	6	14	3	2	2	1
[2.5,3.49]	174	37	87	38	4	4	1	3
[3.5,4.49]	91	33	36	18	4	0	0	0
[4.5,5]	13	5	7	1	0	0	0	0
NA	40	12	19	5	1	0	1	2
Signif	0.00	0.37	0.03	0.36	0.72	0.00	0.09	0.56

Religious practice pray

Those who make prayer their religious practice tend to make better grades than those who do not practice prayer.

Table 12 GPA by Religious practice pray

Joint Frequency	Total	Yes	No
Total	371	261	110
[0,1.5]	11	2	9
[1.6,2.4]	42	18	24
[2.5,3.49]	174	129	45
[3.5,4.49]	91	76	15
[4.5,5]	13	12	1
NA	40	24	16
Significance	0.00	0.05	0.00

Religious practice Mediate

There is not any association between religious practice of meditation and grade point average.

Table 13 GPA by Religious practice Meditate

Joint Frequency	Total	Yes	No
Total	371	67	304
[0,1.5]	11	2	9
[1.6,2.4]	42	10	32
[2.5,3.49]	174	34	140
[3.5,4.49]	91	13	78
[4.5,5]	13	2	11
NA	40	6	34
Significance	1.00	0.92	1.00

Religious practice Deep relaxation

There is not any association between religious practice of deep relaxation and grade point average.

Table 14 GPA by Religious practice Deep relaxation

Joint Frequency	Total	Yes	No
Total	371	35	336
[0,1.5]	11	1	10
[1.6,2.4]	42	6	36
[2.5,3.49]	174	15	159
[3.5,4.49]	91	7	84
[4.5,5]	13	2	11
NA	40	4	36
Significance	1.00	0.92	1.00

Religious practice Contemplate

There is not any association between religious practice of contemplation and grade point average.

Table 15 GPA by Religious practice Contemplate

Joint Frequency	Total	Yes	No
Total	371	35	336
[0,1.5]	11	3	8
[1.6,2.4]	42	3	39
[2.5,3.49]	174	16	158
[3.5,4.49]	91	6	85
[4.5,5]	13	1	12
NA	40	6	34
Significance	0.88	0.41	1.00

Importance of religion in my life

Having religion be extremely important is correlated with having average or near average grades. Significance = 0.05.
Having religion be only somewhat important or not at all important is correlated with poor grades. Significance = 0.00.
However, many students still make average or better grades in spite of not considering religion to be important.

Table 16 GPA by Importance of religion in my life

Joint Freq	Total	Extremely important	Very important	Somewhat important	Not at all important	NA
Total	371	223	104	22	7	15
[0,1.5]	11	2	2	4	3	0
[1.6,2.4]	42	12	17	9	2	2
[2.5,3.49]	174	114	50	1	2	7
[3.5,4.49]	91	63	23	2	0	3
[4.5,5]	13	7	5	1	0	0
NA	40	25	7	5	0	3
Signif	0.00	0.05	0.54	0.00	0.00	0.89

Childhood neighborhood

The Inner city child neighborhood can affect grade point average for students who otherwise would make average grade point average.

Table 17 GPA by Childhood neighborhood

Joint Freq	Total	A city or urban area	Inner city	A suburban area	A small village or town	Rural area	NA
Total	371	167	32	56	40	65	11
[0,1.5]	11	4	1	2	2	2	0
[1.6,2.4]	42	11	10	6	2	13	0
[2.5,3.49]	174	84	7	29	17	32	5
[3.5,4.49]	91	42	7	14	13	14	1
[4.5,5]	13	8	1	0	3	1	0
NA	40	18	6	5	3	3	5
Signif	0.03	0.58	0.01	0.87	0.49	0.26	0.02

Have you ever sold drugs?

Having sold drugs is correlated with making poor grades. However, not having sold drugs is not correlated with making good grades.

Table 18 GPA by Have you ever sold drugs?

Joint Frequency	Total	Yes	No	NA
Total	371	29	332	10
[0,1.5]	11	5	6	0
[1.6,2.4]	42	8	33	1
[2.5,3.49]	174	11	161	2
[3.5,4.49]	91	4	86	1
[4.5,5]	13	0	13	0
NA	40	1	33	6
Significance	0.00	0.00	0.82	0.00

Have you ever belonged to a gang?

There is an association between having belonging to a gang and having poor grades.
However, not belonging to a gang is no assurance that you will make good grades.

Table 19 GPA by Have you ever belonged to a gang?

Joint Frequency	Total	Yes	No	NA
Total	371	23	326	22
[0,1.5]	11	4	7	0
[1.6,2.4]	42	5	32	5
[2.5,3.49]	174	6	163	5
[3.5,4.49]	91	5	82	4
[4.5,5]	13	1	11	1
NA	40	2	31	7
Significance	0.00	0.00	0.86	0.02

How many of your current college close friends regularly smoke cigarettes?

Having all or most close friends smoke cigarettes is associated with making bad grades.

Table 20 GPA by How many of your current college close friends regularly smoke cigarettes?

Joint Freq	Total	All	Most	Many	Some	None	NA
Total	371	4	28	10	90	229	10
[0,1.5]	11	1	3	1	1	5	0
[1.6,2.4]	42	0	8	3	11	20	0
[2.5,3.49]	174	2	9	3	53	106	1
[3.5,4.49]	91	0	5	3	16	64	3
[4.5,5]	13	1	0	0	3	9	0
NA	40	0	3	0	6	25	6
Signif	0.00	0.03	0.01	0.33	0.32	0.80	0.00

How do you think these friends would feel about you smoking cigarettes regularly?

Expecting close friends to approve of one self-smoking cigarettes is associated with low grade point average.

Table 21 GPA by How do you think these friends would feel about you smoking cigarettes regularly?

Joint Freq	Total	Approve	Disapprove	Don't care	NA
Total	371	24	215	93	39
[0,1.5]	11	3	4	4	0
[1.6,2.4]	42	6	16	19	1
[2.5,3.49]	174	10	106	42	16
[3.5,4.49]	91	4	58	20	9
[4.5,5]	13	1	9	2	1
NA	40	0	22	6	12
Signif	0.00	0.02	0.56	0.13	0.00

Do you and your boy or girl friend attend the same college or university?

There is not any association between having boy or girl friend attend same school, and grade point average.

Table 22 GPA by Do you and your boy or girl friend attend the same college or university?

Joint Frequency	Total	Yes	No	NA
Total	371	126	223	22
[0,1.5]	11	5	6	0
[1.6,2.4]	42	11	30	1
[2.5,3.49]	174	62	104	8
[3.5,4.49]	91	30	56	5
[4.5,5]	13	6	7	0
NA	40	12	20	8
Significance	0.33	0.91	0.94	0.01

If you and your boy or girlfriend attend the same college or university, do you live or share an apartment or room together?

Living with your boy or girl friend appears to be significantly correlated with having an extremely low GPA.
Not living with your boy or girlfriend was not significantly correlated with any particular GPA.

Table 23 GPA by If you and your boy or girlfriend attend the same college or university, do you live or share an apartment or room together?

Joint Frequency	Total	Yes	No	NA
Total	371	40	285	46
[0,1.5]	11	6	5	0
[1.6,2.4]	42	6	34	2
[2.5,3.49]	174	17	138	19
[3.5,4.49]	91	6	74	11
[4.5,5]	13	3	9	1
NA	40	2	25	13
Significance	0.00	0.00	0.80	0.01

Do you plan to marry or engage to your boy or girl friend?

There is not any association between intending to marry girl or boy friend, and grade point average.

Table 24 GPA by Do you plan to marry or engage to your boy or girl friend?

Joint Frequency	Total	Yes	No	NA	Married	Maybe
Total	371	149	172	46	3	1
[0,1.5]	11	3	8	0	0	0
[1.6,2.4]	42	14	27	1	0	0
[2.5,3.49]	174	73	78	20	3	0
[3.5,4.49]	91	42	35	13	0	1
[4.5,5]	13	8	5	0	0	0
NA	40	9	19	12	0	0
Significance	0.22	0.37	0.42	0.01	0.76	0.80

Do you always study together with your boy or girl friend?

There is not any association between studying together with boy or girl friend, and grade point average.

Table 25 GPA by Do you always study together with your boy or girl friend?

Joint Frequency	Total	Yes	No	NA	Married
Total	371	104	232	34	1
[0,1.5]	11	2	8	1	0
[1.6,2.4]	42	12	30	0	0
[2.5,3.49]	174	53	106	14	1
[3.5,4.49]	91	21	62	8	0
[4.5,5]	13	4	9	0	0
NA	40	12	17	11	0
Significance	0.32	0.95	0.69	0.00	0.98

If not living together, how many times do you see each other on a daily basis?

There is not any association between how many times each day one sees their boy or girl friend and grade point average.

This question is not well defined because number of times you see your boy or girl friend is not correlated with total time together. You could spend all day with your girlfriend, and it would be correct to say that you see her only once. Or it could be that you see her six times a day, each time for 1 minute between classes.

Table 26 GPA by If not living together, how many times do you see each other on a daily basis?

Joint Freq	Total	One to two times	Two to five times	NA	Other
Total	371	192	51	110	18
[0,1.5]	11	9	1	1	0
[1.6,2.4]	42	28	10	4	0
[2.5,3.49]	174	84	19	58	13
[3.5,4.49]	91	51	13	22	5
[4.5,5]	13	7	3	3	0
NA	40	13	5	22	0
Signif	0.03	0.29	0.52	0.01	0.26

How many times do you and your boy/girlfriend call each other on the telephone?

There is not any association between number of times students calls boy or girl friend and grade point average.
The problem with this question is that you do not know how long they talked each time they called.

Table 27 GPA by How many times do you and your boy/girlfriend call each other on the telephone?

Joint Freq	Total	One to five times daily	Five to ten times daily	Do not call daily, but call weekly	A day after the other	NA
Total	371	157	36	58	77	43
[0,1.5]	11	3	2	1	4	1
[1.6,2.4]	42	24	7	4	7	0
[2.5,3.49]	174	75	16	26	37	20
[3.5,4.49]	91	45	7	18	15	6
[4.5,5]	13	2	2	3	6	0
NA	40	8	2	6	8	16
Signif	0.00	0.09	0.59	0.83	0.37	0.00

What is your area of study in the areas of science and arts?

There is not any association between major study area and grade point average.

Table 28 GPA by What is your area of study in the areas of science and arts?

Joint Frequency	Total	Arts	Science	NA
Total	371	112	231	28
[0,1.5]	11	5	3	3
[1.6,2.4]	42	8	26	8
[2.5,3.49]	174	48	121	5
[3.5,4.49]	91	34	57	0
[4.5,5]	13	4	9	0
NA	40	13	15	12
Significance	0.00	0.60	0.26	0.00

Do you and your boyfriend have a baby together?

Having a baby together appears to be a handicap to making good grades.
However, not having a baby together is not assurance of making good grades.

Table 29 GPA by Do you and your boyfriend have a baby together?

Joint Frequency	Total	Yes	No	NA
Total	371	15	324	32
[0,1.5]	11	4	7	0
[1.6,2.4]	42	5	37	0
[2.5,3.49]	174	5	158	11
[3.5,4.49]	91	1	86	4
[4.5,5]	13	0	11	2
NA	40	0	25	15
Significance	0.00	0.00	0.63	0.00

Do you or your girlfriend have a baby together?

Having a baby together is significantly correlated with low grade point average.

Table 30 GPA by Do you or your girlfriend have a baby together?

Joint Frequency	Total	Yes	No	NA
Total	371	15	300	56
[0,1.5]	11	2	9	0
[1.6,2.4]	42	8	30	4
[2.5,3.49]	174	3	147	24
[3.5,4.49]	91	1	79	11
[4.5,5]	13	1	12	0
NA	40	0	23	17
Significance	0.00	0.00	0.67	0.00

Do you or your girlfriend or boyfriend have a baby for someone else?

You and your boy or girl friend caring for a baby for someone else is not associated with grade point average.

Table 31 GPA by Do you or your girlfriend or boyfriend have a baby for someone else?

Joint Frequency	Total	Yes	No	NA
Total	371	7	328	36
[0,1.5]	11	1	10	0
[1.6,2.4]	42	2	39	1
[2.5,3.49]	174	0	159	15
[3.5,4.49]	91	3	85	3
[4.5,5]	13	0	12	1
NA	40	1	23	16
Significance	0.00	0.15	0.56	0.00

Do you feel that you love your girlfriend vis vis as she you?

There is an association between feeling that love is mutual and grade point average, but only for those students whose grade point average is in the range [3.5, 4.49].

Table 32 GPA by Do you feel that you love your girlfriend vis vis as she you?

Joint Frequency	Total	Yes	No	NA	Other
Total	371	209	110	50	2
[0,1.5]	11	3	8	0	0
[1.6,2.4]	42	17	21	4	0
[2.5,3.49]	174	102	50	21	1
[3.5,4.49]	91	68	16	6	1
[4.5,5]	13	9	4	0	0
NA	40	10	11	19	0
Significance	0.00	0.01	0.01	0.00	0.98

What was your basis for choosing him/her for this intimate friendship?

Those student who said they chose beauty as a basis for intimate friendship are much more like to have made a GPA in the range [1.6,2.4].

Table 33 GPA by What was your basis for choosing him/her for this intimate friendship?

Joint Freq	Total	Intellectual basis	Beauty	NA	Other	No basis
Total	371	235	69	51	15	1
[0,1.5]	11	6	4	1	0	0
[1.6,2.4]	42	19	19	3	1	0
[2.5,3.49]	174	118	28	21	6	1
[3.5,4.49]	91	66	14	5	6	0
[4.5,5]	13	10	1	0	2	0
NA	40	16	3	21	0	0
Signif	0.00	0.25	0.00	0.00	0.23	0.98

How often do you text your boy/girlfriend?

There is not any association between frequency of texting and grade point average.
The misleading significance number of 0.03 is due to 5 students with grade point average in the range of [4.5, 5].
The misleading significance number of 0.08 is due to 13 students for which I did not have grade point average.

Table 34 GPA by How often do you text your boy/girlfriend?

Joint Frequency	Total	Every time, even in class	Once in a while	I do not text	NA
Total	371	46	245	46	34
[0,1.5]	11	3	4	3	1
[1.6,2.4]	42	9	27	6	0
[2.5,3.49]	174	15	129	15	15
[3.5,4.49]	91	9	66	15	1
[4.5,5]	13	5	6	2	0
NA	40	5	13	5	17
Significance	0.00	0.03	0.08	0.99	0.00

How long have you been in this relationship as an intimate one?

There is not any association between length of time of the relationship and grade point average.

The misleading 0.00 significance for the table as a whole is due to the students who did not answer either question.

Table 35 GPA by How long have you been in this relationship as an intimate one?

Joint Freq	Total	Less than a year	One year	Three years	Since high school	NA	Five years	It is not intimate
Total	371	103	73	105	42	45	1	2
[0,1.5]	11	4	2	3	1	1	0	0
[1.6,2.4]	42	18	9	9	6	0	0	0
[2.5,3.49]	174	49	36	49	16	23	0	1
[3.5,4.49]	91	26	15	33	13	4	0	0
[4.5,5]	13	2	4	2	4	0	1	0
NA	40	4	7	9	2	17	0	1
Signif	0.00	0.17	0.96	0.68	0.27	0.00	0.00	0.72

Have you ever been involved in a serious fight in which the police were called?

Those students who have been involved in a fight so severe that police were called are very likely to have made a low grade point average.

Table 36 GPA by Have you ever been involved in a serious fight in which the police were called?

Joint Frequency	Total	Never been involved in such a fight	Yes we did	NA
Total	371	296	44	31
[0,1.5]	11	4	5	2
[1.6,2.4]	42	20	18	4
[2.5,3.49]	174	146	15	13
[3.5,4.49]	91	87	4	0
[4.5,5]	13	11	2	0
NA	40	28	0	12
Significance	0.00	0.07	0.00	0.00

Do you and your girl/boyfriend use alcohol, that is, drink beer, wine, or liquor?

Use of alcohol is correlated with low grades, unless the use is in moderation.

Table 37 GPA by Do you and your girl/boyfriend use alcohol, that is, drink beer, wine, or liquor?

Joint Frequency	Total	Yes	No	Sometimes	NA
Total	371	63	220	59	29
[0,1.5]	11	7	3	1	0
[1.6,2.4]	42	19	17	5	1
[2.5,3.49]	174	22	104	34	14
[3.5,4.49]	91	12	63	14	2
[4.5,5]	13	1	10	2	0
NA	40	2	23	3	12
Significance	0.00	0.00	0.36	0.68	0.00

If you see somebody cheating with your boy/girlfriend, will you use deadly force on your friend or both of them?

Saying you would use deadly force against someone cheating with your boy or girl friend, is correlated with making low grades.

Table 38 GPA by If you see somebody cheating with your boy/girlfriend, will you use deadly force on your friend or both of them?

Joint Frequency	Total	Yes	No	NA
Total	371	50	289	32
[0,1.5]	11	7	4	0
[1.6,2.4]	42	17	25	0
[2.5,3.49]	174	15	141	18
[3.5,4.49]	91	10	80	1
[4.5,5]	13	1	12	0
NA	40	0	27	13
Significance	0.00	0.00	0.36	0.00

Do you think your boy/girlfriend can be of influence in your life regarding decision making?

Not expecting your boy or girl friend to be able to help you make life decisions is correlated with making low grades.

Table 39 GPA by Do you think your boy/girlfriend can be of influence in your life regarding decision making?

Joint Frequency	Total	Yes	No	NA
Total	371	229	113	29
[0,1.5]	11	3	8	0
[1.6,2.4]	42	22	20	0
[2.5,3.49]	174	117	43	14
[3.5,4.49]	91	63	27	1
[4.5,5]	13	8	5	0
NA	40	16	10	14
Significance	0.00	0.28	0.04	0.00

Do you want to influence your friend for your betterment?

Not wanting to influence your friend for your betterment is correlated with low grades.
However, it is likely that many students misread this question to be asking about influencing their friend for the friend's betterment.

Table 40 GPA by Do you want to influence your friend for your betterment?

Joint Frequency	Total	Yes	No	NA
Total	371	251	91	29
[0,1.5]	11	3	8	0
[1.6,2.4]	42	24	17	1
[2.5,3.49]	174	119	43	12
[3.5,4.49]	91	73	18	0
[4.5,5]	13	10	2	1
NA	40	22	3	15
Significance	0.00	0.36	0.00	0.00

Do you feel emotionally attached to your friend?

Not feeling emotionally attached to your boy or girl friend, is correlated with low grades.

Table 41 GPA by Do you feel emotionally attached to your friend?

Joint Frequency	Total	Yes	No	NA
Total	371	244	99	28
[0,1.5]	11	2	8	1
[1.6,2.4]	42	22	19	1
[2.5,3.49]	174	123	41	10
[3.5,4.49]	91	70	20	1
[4.5,5]	13	11	2	0
NA	40	16	9	15
Significance	0.00	0.06	0.00	0.00

Does your friend discuss all his/her problems and issues with you?

Students who made low grades tended to answer no to this question, and students who made high grades tended to answer yes to this question.

Table 42 GPA by Does your friend discuss all his/her problems and issues with you?

Joint Frequency	Total	Yes	No	NA
Total	371	220	118	33
[0,1.5]	11	4	7	0
[1.6,2.4]	42	17	23	2
[2.5,3.49]	174	105	53	16
[3.5,4.49]	91	74	17	0
[4.5,5]	13	8	5	0
NA	40	12	13	15
Significance	0.00	0.01	0.02	0.00

Have either of you purchased an engagement ring for the other?

Having bought an engagement ring for your boy or girl friend is correlated with low grade point average.

Table 43 GPA by Have either of you purchased an engagement ring for the other?

Joint Frequency	Total	Yes	No	NA
Total	371	70	267	34
[0,1.5]	11	6	4	1
[1.6,2.4]	42	13	29	0
[2.5,3.49]	174	32	127	15
[3.5,4.49]	91	9	80	2
[4.5,5]	13	6	7	0
NA	40	4	20	16
Significant	0.00	0.0	0.20	0.00

REFERENCES

Ask.com (2014). "*What Is the Meaning of Theoretical Framework?*". Retrieved from http://www.ask.com/question/what-is-the-meaning-of-theoretical-framework

Babaeva, (2010). *Russia now*. Retrieved from http://russianow.washingtonpost.com/2010/05/what-does-friendship-mean-to-a-russian.php

Burbach C. (2014). Cherie Burbach *Faith Words Relationships* retrieved from http://cherieburbach.com/

BURBACH, C. E. B. H. J., & CNAAN, R. (1983). *DISCONTINUITY IN SOCIAL NETWORKS OF UNDERGRADUATE SOCIAL WORK STUDENTS: A PART OF PROFESSIONAL RE-SOCIALIZATION.*Sociology Toward the Year 2000: The Sociological Galaxy, 189.

Conger, John Janeway; Galambos, Nancy (1997).*Adolescence and youth: psychological development in a changing world* (5th ed. ed.). New York: Longman.ISBN 978-0-673-99262-8.

Costello, Bob (2009). *The Restorative Practices Handbook*. Pennsylvania: International Institute for Restorative Practices. pp. 71–72.

Dalton, M. (1959)*Men Who Manage*, New York: Wiley.

(Daniel, 2008; Miller, Rowland and Perlman, (eds Daniel, 2008) Retrieved from http://www.ebay.com/itm/Intimate-Relationships-by-Daniel-Perlman-Rowland-S-Miller-and-Susan-Mille-/231222619034?pt=US_Texbook_Education&hash=item35d5f12b9a

Dunbar, R.I.M. (1992) *Neocortex size as a constraint on group size in primates*. Journal of Human Evolution, Volume 22, Issue 6, Pages 469-493

English Dictionary (2014) retrieved from
http://dictionary.reference.com/

"Definition for friend". *Oxford Dictionaries*. Oxford Dictionary
Press. Retrieved 25 May 2012.

Forster. "*Is Science Value-Free?*" Retrieved from
http://philosophy.wisc.edu/forster/220/notes_7.html

Fuller, D. (2011). *Long-Term, Intimate Partnerships can promote
unhealthy habits*. Retrieved from
http://www.uc.edu/news/NR.aspx?id=14061

Grabmeier, J. (January 6, 2004).*Friendships play key role in suicidal
thoughts of girls, but not boys*. Ohio State University.

Islam and the concept of friendship (2012)
"Islam & the Concept of Friendship". Mission Islam. Retrieved 10
June 2012

Jñanavira, Dharmachari (2010). "*Homosexuality in the Japanese
Buddhist Tradition*". Western Buddhist Review 3. Retrieved from
http://www.westernbuddhistreview.com/vol3/homosexuality.html

Kakabadse, A., Kakabadse, N. (2004) *Intimacy: International Survey
of the Sex Lives of People at Work*, Basingstoke: Palgrave

Katja Maria Vogt, katjavogt.com, Columbia University "*The Good
of Others: A Stoic Reading of Plato*". Retrieved from
http://www.katjavogt.com/pdf/katja_vogt_cosmopolitanism.pdf

Khaleque, A. (2004). *Intimate Adult Relationships, Quality of Life
and Psychological Adjustment*. Social Indicators Research, 69, 351-
360.

Kornblum, Janet (June 22, 2006). Study: *25% of Americans have no
one to confide in*. USA Today. retrieved from
http://usatoday30.usatoday.com/news/nation/2006-06-22-
friendship_x.htm

LITRE (2014) NC State University. "*Survey Research*", Retrieved from http://litre.ncsu.edu/sltoolkit/SurveysHow.html

Liz Lampkin(May 19, 2012). "How I Learned To Stop Giving Boyfriends Husband Privileges". Retrieved from http://madamenoire.com/178488/how-i-learned-to-stop-giving-boyfriends-husband-privileges/

Lowe, S. R., Rhodes, J. E., & Scoglio, A. A. (2012). "*Psychology of Women Quarterly*, 36", 286-300. doi: 10.1177/0361684311434307

McPherson, Smith-Lovin, Brashears (Volume 71, Number 3, June 2006). Asanet.org American Sociological Review. Retrieved from http://asr.sagepub.com/content/71/3/353.full.pdf+html

Miller, Rowland & Perlman, Daniel (2008). *Intimate Relationships* (5th ed.). McGraw-Hill. ISBN 978-0-07-337018-7

Mills, J., Clark, K. (1982) "*Exchange and communal relationships*" in L. Wheeler (ed) Review of personality and social psychology (Vol III), Beverly Hills: Sage.

Mission Islam (2012). "*Islam & the Concept of Friendship*". Retrieved http://www.missionislam.com/knowledge/Friendship.htm

Modern-Day Dunbar's number-network 209 wiki, (2004) Retrieved from http://scenic.princeton.edu/network20q/wiki/index.php?title=The_Modern-Day_Dunbar%27s_Number

Monroe, W.S. (1898). *Discussion and reports. Social consciousness in children*. Psychological Review, 15, 68–70

Nathanson D. (1987). *Shame and Pride: Affect, Sex, and the Birth of the Self.* New York. W. W. Norton and Company. ISBN 0-393-31109-0

Nees, G. (2000). *Germany: Unraveling an Enigma*. Intercultural Press. pp. 66–68. ISBN 9781877864759.

Owen, Terence (1996). *Aristotle: Introductory Readings*. Hackett. p. 274.

Oxford University (2008) Oxford American Large Print Dictionary. Oxford University Press. IBSN 978-0-19-537125-3

Radwan,, N. (2012) *"Arab Friendship"*. Fact of Arabs. Retrieved 10 from http://www.factofarabs.net/ERA.aspx?Id=345&TID=7

Reczek, Corinne, Assistant Professor in the Department of Sociology at the University of Cincinnati. "*The Promotion of Unhealthy Habits in Gay, Lesbian, and Straight Intimate Partnerships*". Tue, Aug 23, 2011 - 12:30pm - 2:10pm. 106th Annual Meeting of the American Sociological Association. Retrieved Aug 26, 2011.

Research Methods Knowledge Base (2014) "Survey Research" Retrieved from http://www.socialresearchmethods.net/kb/survey.php

Ridley-Duff, R.J. (2005) "*Interpersonal Dynamics: A Communitarian Perspective*", paper to the 1st ENROAC-MCA Conference 7th–9th April, Antwerp.

Said, E. (1979). Orientalism. United States: Vintage Books. p. Chapter 2: *Orientalist Structures and Restructures*. ISBN 978-0-394-74067-6. ISBN 0-394-74067-X.

Simon, M. K.,Goes J. (2011) "*Developing a theoretical framework*". Retrieved from http://drannejonesuas.files.wordpress.com/2013/10/recipe-for-a-theoretical-framework.pdf

Stanford Encyclopedia of Philosophy (2013) Friendship Retrieved from http://plato.stanford.edu/entries/friendship/

Stout (2010)
Structures and Restructures. ISBN 978-0-394-74067-6. ISBN 0-394-74067-X.

Susan Combs, Texas Comptroller of Public Accounts (2014). Texas School Performance Review (TSPR). Retrieved from http://www.window.state.tx.us/tspr/

Tokar, Alexander (2009). *Metaphors of the Web 2.0: with special emphasis on social networks and folksonomies.* Frankfurt: Peter Lang. p. 57. ISBN 3631586647.

Wikipedia (2014) "*Friendship*". Retrieved from http://en.wikipedia.org/wiki/Friendship

Wikipedia (2014) "*Intimate Relationship*" Retrieved from http://en.wikipedia.org/wiki/Intimate_relationship
Willis, Amy (2011). "*Most adults have 'only two close friends'*". London: The Telegraph. Retrieved from http://www.telegraph.co.uk/technology/facebook/8876376/Most-adults-have-only-two-close-friends.html

Williams, Alex (15 July 2012). "*Why Is It Hard to Make Friends Over 30?*". The New York Times. Retrieved from http://www.nytimes.com/2012/07/15/fashion/the-challenge-of-making-friends-as-an-adult.html?pagewanted=all&_r=0

The World Bank (2014) *Quantifying Environmental Performance Survey Results.* Retrieved from http://econ.worldbank.org/WBSITE/EXTERNAL/EXTDEC/EXTRESEARCH/0,,contentMDK:20761754~pagePK:64214825~piPK:64214943~theSitePK:469382,00.html

www.ingramcontent.com/pod-product-compliance
Lightning Source LLC
Chambersburg PA
CBHW060202290526
45789CB00003B/1128